W9-BAT-018

This Book Is Dedicated To

## MACKENZIE HONNICK

who journeyed
around the world
by reading at the
Totowa Public Library!

Summer 2011

16    Total Books
Read

4/28/2005

Grades 3-6

# Festivals *of the* World

# SCOTLAND

Gareth Stevens Publishing
MILWAUKEE

DWIGHT D. EISENHOWER LIBRARY
537 TOTOWA ROAD
TOTOWA BOROUGH, N.J. 07512

Written by
JONATHAN GRIFFITHS

Edited by
GERALDINE MESENAS

Designed by
LOO CHUAN MING

Picture research by
SUSAN JANE MANUEL

First published in North America in 1999 by
**Gareth Stevens Publishing**
1555 North RiverCenter Drive, Suite 201
Milwaukee, Wisconsin 53212 USA

For a free color catalog describing Gareth
Stevens' list of high-quality books and multimedia
programs, call
1-800-542-2595 (USA)
or 1-800-461-9120 (Canada).
Gareth Stevens Publishing's Fax: (414) 225-0377.

All rights reserved. No part of this book may be
reproduced or utilized in any form or by any
means electronic or mechanical, including
photocopying, recording, or by an information
storage and retrieval system, without permission
from the copyright owner.

© TIMES EDITIONS PTE LTD 1999
Originated and designed by
Times Books International
an imprint of Times Editions Pte Ltd
Times Centre, 1 New Industrial Road
Singapore 536196
Printed in Malaysia

**Library of Congress Cataloging-in-Publication Data:**
Griffiths, Jonathan.
Scotland / by Jonathan Griffiths.
p.  cm. — (Festivals of the world)
Includes bibliographical references and index.
Summary: Describes how the culture of Scotland is
reflected in its many festivals, including
Up-Helly-Aa, the Highland Games, and the
Edinburgh Military Tattoo.
ISBN 0-8368-2034-7 (lib. bdg.)
1. Festivals—Scotland—Juvenile literature.
2. Scotland—Social life and customs—Juvenile
literature. [1. Festivals—Scotland. 2. Holidays—
Scotland. 3. Scotland—Social life and customs.]
I. Title. II. Series.
GT4844.A2G75    1999
394.269411—dc21          99-18091

1 2 3 4 5 6 7 8 9 03 02 01 00 99

# CONTENTS

# It's Festival Time . . .

S cotland celebrates many annual events in which tradition and fun are major features. Whether they are dressed up as Vikings in Up-Helly-Aa, tossing the caber at the Highland Games, or playing the bagpipes at the Edinburgh Military Tattoo, the Scots always put on a good show. So, don a tartan plaid and join us. It's festival time in Scotland!

# WHERE'S SCOTLAND?

Scotland is one of four countries that make up the United Kingdom. The others are England, Northern Ireland, and Wales. Scotland is a mountainous country, famous for its beautiful Highlands, lakes, and rivers. It has an area of 30,418 square miles (78,783 square kilometers). It also has nearly 800 islands off its rugged coastline. The capital city of Scotland is Edinburgh [ed-in-BRUH].

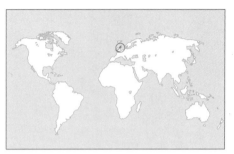

## Who are the Scots?

Most Scottish people descend from the **Celts** [KELTS], who came to Scotland more than 2,000 years ago. A popular image of Scotland is the Highlander, wearing a tartan kilt and playing the bagpipes. People dress as Highlanders in many Scottish festivals today.

English is the official language of Scotland, although it might sound like a different language because of the strong Scottish accent. **Gaelic**, an ancient Celtic language, is also spoken in some areas, especially in the Highlands.

These Scottish girls will compete in one of the many exciting events at the Edinburgh Highland Games.

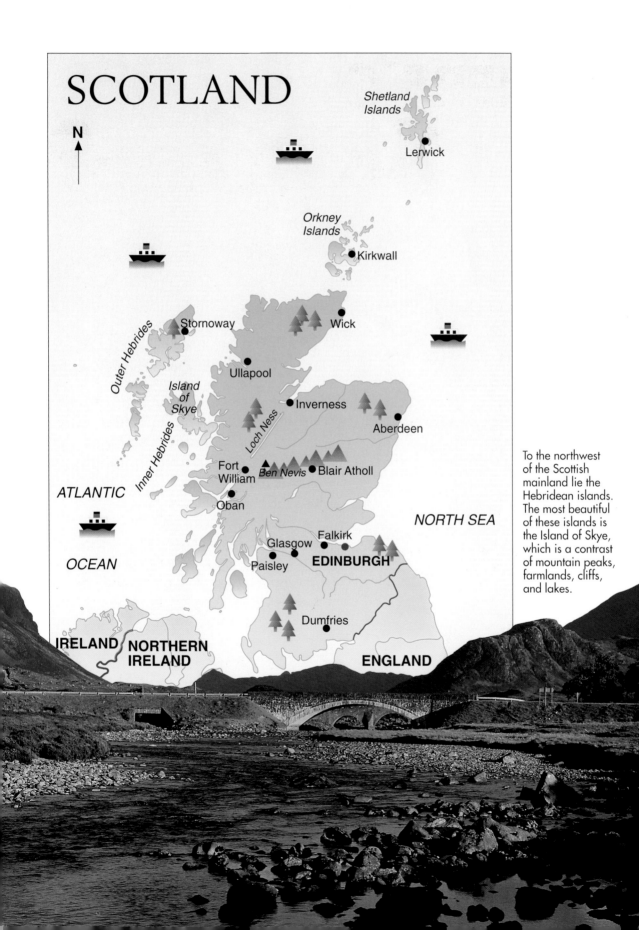

# SCOTLAND

N

*Shetland Islands*

Lerwick

*Orkney Islands*

Kirkwall

*Outer Hebrides*

Stornoway

Wick

Ullapool

*Island of Skye*

Inverness

*Loch Ness*

Aberdeen

*Inner Hebrides*

Fort William

*Ben Nevis*

Blair Atholl

ATLANTIC

Oban

NORTH SEA

OCEAN

Glasgow

Falkirk

Paisley

EDINBURGH

Dumfries

IRELAND

NORTHERN IRELAND

ENGLAND

To the northwest of the Scottish mainland lie the Hebridean islands. The most beautiful of these islands is the Island of Skye, which is a contrast of mountain peaks, farmlands, cliffs, and lakes.

# WHEN'S THE PARTY?

> Read on to learn more about Highlanders, bagpipes, and tartan plaid.

## SPRING

- ✪ **EASTER**—This Christian festival celebrates not only the resurrection of Jesus Christ, but also the arrival of spring.
- ✪ **EDINBURGH FOLK FESTIVAL**—This festival celebrates Scottish heritage.
- ✪ **APRIL FOOLS' DAY**—On this day, people play practical jokes on each other. Some towns even have a procession of fools.
- ✪ **BELTANE FIRE FESTIVAL**
- ✪ **MAY DAY**—Traditional May Day celebrations include dancing around the Maypole.

## SUMMER

- ✪ **RIDING OF THE MARCHES**— Celebrated in Scotland's border towns, with parades of pipe bands, this festival commemorates the wars between the Scots and the English.
- ✪ **HIGHLAND GAMES**
- ✪ **EDINBURGH INTERNATIONAL FESTIVAL AND FRINGE**
- ✪ **EDINBURGH MILITARY TATTOO**

## AUTUMN

✪ **BEN NEVIS RACE**—In this event, Scots race to the top of Ben Nevis and back. At 4,406 feet (1,343 meters), Ben Nevis is the highest mountain in Scotland.

✪ **THE NATIONAL MOD**—This October festival includes contests in all aspects of Gaelic performing arts.

✪ **GLENFIDDICH PIPING CHAMPIONSHIPS**—The world's top ten solo pipers compete at Blair Atholl in October.

## WINTER

✪ **CHRISTMAS DAY**

✪ **BOXING DAY**

✪ **HOGMANAY (NEW YEAR'S EVE) AND NEW YEAR'S DAY**—This holiday is more important to the Scots than Christmas. According to tradition, they visit their neighbors at midnight on New Year's Eve, and the first person to step into the house should be dark-haired and carrying a basket containing coal, salt, and whiskey.

✪ **STONEHAVEN FIREBALL CEREMONY**—On January 1st, people swing long sticks with fireballs at the ends to ward off evil spirits and usher in the New Year.

✪ **UP-HELLY-AA**

✪ **BURNS NIGHT**—On January 25th, Scotland honors its greatest poet, Robert Burns, with traditional Scottish food and poetry recitals.

*How do you like my Viking costume? See other Scots dressed like Vikings in the Up-Helly-Aa fire festival on pages 20–23.*

# HIGHLAND GAMES

Nothing is more Scottish than the Highland Games. At the Games, Scots celebrate all things unique to their culture and heritage as they compete in traditional piping, dancing, and sporting contests. The Highland Games bring people together and keep the traditions of Scotland alive.

## Gathering of the Clans

The Highland Games are also called the "Gathering of the Clans." A clan is a family group, the members of which share a common ancestor. A long time ago, each clan even had its own tartan, or heavy woven cloth with a distinctive plaid pattern. The clans would gather to air their differences and pit their members against members of the other clans in contests of strength, music, and dancing. Although, these days, the Highland Games are not hostile, they are still fiercely competitive.

The Highland Games include Scottish heavy events, Highland dancing, bagpipes, drumming, and traditional Scottish food.

This young girl has mastered the complicated steps of a Highland dance.

The drum major of a pipe band stands tall in his traditional Scottish costume.

*Above:* Pipe bands compete in the Highland Games, playing traditional Scottish music.

# Bagpipes and drumming

In the 19th century, Highland regiments formed bagpipe and drum bands. Today, pipe bands are featured in many Scottish festivals.

Competitors at the Highland Games' piping competitions are judged on their piping skills and their ability to play stirring, traditional Scottish music. Drummers play marches in the drumming competitions. The marches become quicker and more difficult as the music progresses. Hearing the drums getting quicker and quicker, as the drummers do their best to impress the judges, is exciting.

Pipers play throughout the Highland Games. Bagpipes are steeped in tradition, and players take the history of the pipes seriously. Playing the pipes is a lifetime commitment; many people spend their whole lives learning to play. At the Games, they not only compete with other pipers, but they also can learn new ways of playing by meeting other pipers. There are piping competitions for children, too. Really good bagpipe players usually start young.

9

# Highland dancing

The Highland dance competition is one of the children's favorite events at the Highland Games. Highland dancing requires great concentration because the steps become faster and more complicated as the dance progresses. Many of the competitors are young girls and boys, who perform the complex steps of Highland dances with incredible skill. The two main Highland dances are the fling and the sword dance.

The Highland fling began as a victory dance following a battle. A solo dancer performs with raised arms, kicking with his or her feet over a small area.

The Highland sword dance is extremely popular at the Games. A group dances around swords placed on the ground, taking care not to touch any of the swords. The dancers are amazing to watch as they move in and out of the pattern of swords without missing a step.

Children perform the difficult steps of the Highland sword dance as they compete at the Highland Games.

10

# Scottish heavy events

For a lot of people, the heavy events are the highlight of the Highland Games. The contestants in the heavy events exhibit remarkable strength. The most famous event is the caber toss. A caber is similar to a tree trunk. It is 12 to 19 feet (4 to 6 m) long and weighs between 30 and 120 pounds (14 and 54 kilograms). A contestant picks up the caber and rests it against his shoulder. Then, he pushes it upward and lets it go. The winner is the contestant who tosses the caber the farthest. Strength, timing, and balance all play a part. In the weight for height event, contestants try to throw a weight as high as possible over a bar. Weight for distance is a similar game, but the contestants try to throw the weight as far as possible. Another event, called the stone put, is similar to a track-and-field event known as the shot put.

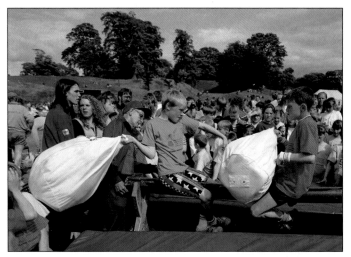

Two boys are battling it out in one of the less traditional events at the Highland Games in Falkirk.

This strong Scotsman prepares to fling a tremendous weight in the heavy events at the Highland Games.

## Think about this

The Highland Games celebrate being Scottish more than any other festival in Scotland. They teach modern Scots about their heritage and help preserve many of the old traditions. Scotland is an old country with ancient traditions, and, although it is now part of the United Kingdom, it still celebrates its own history and identity. Scottish children are fortunate to be able to learn so much about the history of their country by attending one festival—the Highland Games.

# EDINBURGH INTERNATIONAL FESTIVAL AND FRINGE

T he Edinburgh International Festival is one of the world's largest and most important arts celebrations. It was first held in 1947 and has since become a showcase for some of the world's best performing artists and musicians. The Fringe Festival features performers not included in the main festival, and it is much larger than the main festival. The population of Edinburgh swells to bursting as people from all over the world visit to sample the arts on display in the Scottish capital.

*Above:* Talented, colorful mimes provide laughs at the Edinburgh International Festival.

*Left:* The opening ceremony of the Edinburgh International Festival is an exciting and lively display.

*Opposite:* Young street performers entertain the crowds at the Fringe Festival.

*Left:* The Edinburgh International Festival offers many elegant dance performances.

*Below:* A member of the Children's Theater Troupe plays a dramatic role in the Fringe Festival.

# Bringing the world to Scotland

For three weeks every August, the Edinburgh International Festival is one of Scotland's major tourist attractions. It features drama, music, dance, and opera and encourages children to participate in and learn more about the arts.

When the first festival was planned in 1947, the objective was to promote peace after World War II. The festival was a success and, more than 50 years later, continues to grow, attracting more and more people each year. Visitors can choose from approximately 75 different shows.

Since Scotland has suffered over the years from a high rate of unemployment, events such as the Edinburgh International Festival provide jobs for the local people and help the city's economy.

# The Fringe Festival

The largest arts festival in the world has something for everyone, and there are no restrictions on who can perform. Hundreds of shows are offered, and every available space is used by performers. At the Fringe, audience members take a chance on what they will see, because most of the shows are brand-new or have not been seen by many people before.

The Fringe began when eight theater companies arrived at the Edinburgh International Festival uninvited. These companies performed in small buildings on the edge of that festival. The Fringe got its name when a journalist described these productions as "the fringe of the official festival drama." Today, over 500 companies deliver thousands of performances at the Fringe, which usually starts about a week before the Edinburgh International Festival, because there are so many shows to fit in.

At the Fringe, many performances are held outdoors, in parks and on the streets. Some Fringe performers entertain in the schools.

### Think about this
Besides the Fringe, several other festivals have developed alongside the Edinburgh International Festival. One of the more popular is the Edinburgh International Film Festival, which features noteworthy films, offers filmmaking classes, and affords many opportunities to meet actors and film makers. At this time of year, there is little doubt that Edinburgh is the festival capital of the world!

# EDINBURGH MILITARY TATTOO

One of the most spectacular festivals in Scotland is the Edinburgh Military Tattoo. It originally began as the Scottish army's contribution to the Edinburgh International Festival. It has since become one of the world's greatest shows, a unique blend of military bands, ceremony, and fireworks. The Edinburgh Military Tattoo is a very Scottish event, with bagpipes and kilted Scottish regiments taking center stage. It is held on the grounds of Edinburgh Castle, where it is viewed by over 200,000 people.

*Left:* The most accomplished bagpipe players probably start at about the same age as this young piper.

*Below:* A bagpipe band performs in the Edinburgh Military Tattoo.

# The origin of the Tattoo

The word *tattoo* has an interesting origin. In the 17th and 18th centuries, the local army regiment would march through town playing bagpipes and drums to signal soldiers in taverns, or bars, that it was time to return to the barracks. On hearing the music of the pipes and drums, the owners of taverns would shout, "Doe den tap toe," which means "Turn off the taps." "Taps" referred to the beer taps. Gradually, "tap toe" became "tattoo," and, now, any performance of military music is called a tattoo.

    Most of the players at the Edinburgh Military Tattoo are from regular army battalions, which means they are soldiers first and musicians second. Many of them attend the Army School of Bagpipe Music at Edinburgh Castle, so, when they play in the Tattoo, they are on familiar ground.

This female bagpipe player enjoys harmonizing with the rest of the pipe band.

# Music—the heart of the Tattoo

Military and **civilian** bands from all over the world take part in the Edinburgh Military Tattoo held on the Edinburgh Castle **esplanade**. The Tattoo provides entertainment for people of all ages. It is one of the best places to hear bagpipe bands perform and to see demonstrations of military precision in marching and drills. There are also animal performances, gymnastics displays, daredevil stunts, and traditional and modern music and dance performances.

Music is the heart of the Tattoo. All displays are set to music, and pipe and drum bands highlight the festivities. The music of bagpipes is the music of Scotland. Whether this traditional Scottish instrument is played by large pipe bands or a lone piper, the sound of bagpipes is sure to touch the heart of every Scot— and many others besides. With such a wonderful mix of music, excitement, and tradition, it is no wonder the Edinburgh Military Tattoo draws the biggest crowds of any festival in Scotland.

### Think about this
Bagpipes are, perhaps, the objects most often associated with Scotland. Bagpipes did not, however, originate in Scotland. There is evidence that these instruments were used in ancient Persia, Egypt, and Greece. After the Romans introduced them to the English, bagpipes became very popular in Scotland. Clan chiefs adopted them, and they were used as military instruments. Can you think of any products that seem distinctive to your country but actually originated in another country?

*Opposite* and *right:* Scottish military regiments form a dazzling display on the Edinburgh Castle esplanade.

# UP-HELLY-AA

On the last Tuesday in January, normal life in the Shetland Islands town of Lerwick comes to a standstill as the whole town celebrates Britain's biggest and most spectacular fire festival, called Up-Helly-Aa. Each year, almost 1,000 people participate in the Up-Helly-Aa procession, marching behind a large Viking longship. The rest of the townspeople line the streets to see the torchbearers in their elaborate costumes. Many spectators follow the procession to the King George V playing field, where the longship is set ablaze by almost a thousand torches. Up-Helly-Aa celebrates Shetland's Viking heritage and provides a glimpse into the history of Scotland's northern islands.

Dressed in elaborate costumes, the Guizer Jarl and his Viking squad lead the Up-Helly-Aa celebrations.

The leader of the junior squad stands proudly in full Viking gear.

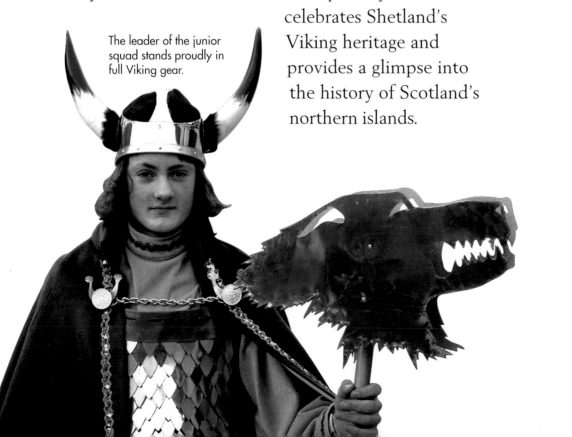

# Shetland's Viking past

Norsemen, or Vikings, from Norway invaded Scotland's northern islands, the Shetland Islands and the Orkney Islands, in the eighth century A.D. With some of the most advanced ships and **navigational** equipment of that time, the Vikings quickly took control of Shetland, Orkney, the western islands, and a small portion of northeast Scotland, all of which remained under Norse control for over six centuries.

During this period, the northern islands of Shetland and Orkney developed distinctively from the rest of Scotland. Norse culture became **prevalent**. Its influence can be seen in beautiful buildings, such as St. Magnus Cathedral in Orkney, which is an excellent example of Norse architecture.

In the fourteenth century, Norse power decreased. Scotland regained control over Orkney in 1468 and Shetland in 1469. Although the northern islands remain part of Scotland today, their Viking heritage is still evident in dialect, culture, and even place names.

The Guizer Jarl squad, in Viking costumes, reenacts Shetland's Viking past.

# The procession

Up-Helly-Aa festivities begin at around seven in the evening with a procession down the streets of Lerwick to a burning site at the King George V playing field. The procession's almost one thousand participants, called guizers, are dressed in elaborate and bizarre costumes. The name *guizer* is derived from the word *disguise*.

At the front of the procession is a large replica of a Viking longship with the head of a dragon on its bow. This ship takes almost four months to build. A squad of men in traditional Viking costumes, complete with winged or horned helmets, shields, silver axes, swords, and capes, walks behind the longship, carrying flaming torches. This squad is headed by the annually-appointed Guizer Jarl, who leads the Up-Helly-Aa festivities. Following the Guizer Jarl's squad are over 40 other squads in costumes ranging from court jesters to cowboys.

Some townspeople watch the procession from the sides of the streets; others wait for the procession at the burning site. All the people are in high spirits as they await the evening's fiery **climax**.

The Guizer Jarl's squad looks on as more and more men join in burning the longship.

Procession participants surround the Viking longship and wait for a signal to throw their torches into the galley.

# Burning the dragon

When the Viking longship is placed in the middle of the King George V playing field, an orange **aura** starts to glow, as almost a thousand guizers encircle the ship with their flaming torches. At around eight in the evening, when the last guizer joins the group, a bugle is sounded, and the guizers shout three cheers—one for the longship builders and torch makers, one for Up-Helly-Aa, and one for the Guizer Jarl. After the cheers, all the guizers throw their torches into the ship, which is quickly engulfed in flames.

The guizer squads then visit town halls, where they perform dances, songs, and plays to entertain the townspeople through the night. The men and women of the town usually prepare food and drink in advance to welcome the guizers to the town halls.

At a signal from the Guizer Jarl, all guizers hurl their flaming torches into the Viking longship.

### Think about this

The Up-Helly-Aa festival is fairly young. It was first introduced only in the 19th century. It is believed to have replaced an older Christmas tradition that involved burning tar barrels and other riotous activities. Town authorities restricted these dangerous activities around 1870, so the townspeople created a new festival with a torchlight procession and fancy dress. They called this new festival Up-Helly-Aa.

# BELTANE FIRE FESTIVAL

Each year, on the night of April 30th, 10 to 12 thousand people gather on Calton Hill in Edinburgh for the Beltane Fire Festival. This festival was first organized in the mid-1980s. Today, it is famous for its elaborate floats and costumes. Everyone in Edinburgh looks forward to this festival's remarkable two-hour procession and the party afterward.

*Right:* Scots welcome the summer with beautiful paper sculptures of the sun.

## Celtic roots

Also known as May Eve and Walpurgis Night, the Beltane Fire Festival reenacts an ancient **pagan** Celtic fire ritual that celebrates the coming of summer. The highlight of the festivities is a procession, which features over 200 performers and drummers. Thousands of people, with flaming torches in their hands, **congregate** at Calton Hill on the night of April 30th to watch the Beltane procession.

A young Scotsman gets a better view of the Beltane procession on his mother's shoulders.

# The Beltane procession

The Beltane Fire Festival begins with the announcement of the annually-appointed May Queen, who then leads the procession with her **entourage** of handmaidens and attendants. On its way to Calton Hill, the procession moves through four points, each representing one of the four elements—water, earth, air, and fire. A small ritual is performed at each point. Drummers, dancers, actors, and fire performers entertain the crowds along the way.

The climax of the procession is the transition from winter to summer, which is visually represented by the death and rebirth of the Green Man, who represents nature. The May Queen then lights the Beltane fire, heralding the arrival of summer. The fire symbolizes the sun, which removes the darkness and suffering of winter. Traditionally, people ran through the fire for good luck.

For the rest of the night, people enjoy themselves—feasting, dancing, and singing, sometimes until the break of dawn.

The May Queen's white handmaidens protect her from evil red devils that represent chaos and disharmony.

# THINGS FOR YOU TO DO

Elements of Highland culture, especially bagpipes and tartan kilts, are the things most people identify as "Scottish." In about 1746, the English banned Highland dress and bagpipe music when the Highlanders revolted against English authority. Only in 1782 was this prohibition lifted. Today, tartan and bagpipes are features of many important Scottish festivals.

## Bagpipe symphony

Bagpipes are the musical instruments most distinctive to Scotland. These ancient instruments consist of an air-filled bag and three kinds of pipes— a blow pipe, a chanter to make melodious sounds, and drones that produce a continuous note. The air in the bag is released through the pipes to make sounds. The piper must continually blow into the bag to replace the air, while, at the same time, covering and uncovering the holes on the pipes to produce the sounds.

Long ago, bagpipes were used by Scottish Highlanders to signal troops. Today, many children are in pipe bands, where they learn the traditional music of Scotland.

# How to wear a tartan plaid

The image of a Scottish piper wearing a tartan kilt is a familiar one. Traditionally, Highlanders wore tartan plaids, or large pieces of cloth wrapped over the shoulder, to keep warm in freezing Highland weather. Today, the Scottish traditional costume includes both kilts and plaids. Wearing a plaid used to be an extremely complicated process. Traditionally, a plaid consisted of up to 16 yards (14.6 meters) of tartan!

You can dress like a Highlander, too! Take a large piece of cloth, preferably of a tartan material, and ask an adult to pin one end of the cloth to your left shoulder. Bring the other end across your back and under your right arm. Then bring it back, across your chest, up to your left shoulder. Secure the plaid to your left shoulder with a **brooch**, and let the rest of the plaid hang over your left shoulder. Now you look like a Highlander!

## Things to look for in your library

*In the Tradition of. . . Scotland.* (http://members.tripod.com/~scotland_98/).
*The Last Piper.* Helen Cavanagh (Simon & Schuster/Juvenile, 1996).
*Little House in the Highlands.* Melissa Peterson (HarperCollins, 1999).
*Scotland Kings and Queens.* Elizabeth Douglas (Seven Hills Book Distributors, 1998).
*Scottish Clans and Tartans. Looking into the Past* (series). Dwayne E. Pickels (Chelsea House Publishing, 1997).
*Scottish Fairy Tales.* Donald A. Mackenzie (Dover Publications, 1997).
*The Vikings in Scotland.* Gordon Jarvie (Seven Hills Book Distributors, 1998).

# MAKE TARTAN

Tartan is one of the best known symbols of Scotland. It is usually made of a thick woolen material. A tartan kilt kept Highlanders warm in freezing Highland weather. Tartan patterns have crisscrossing colored bands or stripes woven into them. The most commonly used colors are red, green, and blue. You can design your own tartan to wear as a kilt or a sash.

**You will need:**

1. Ruler
2. Masking tape, 1" (2.5 cm) wide
3. Pencil
4. Paint roller, 1" (2.5 cm) wide
5. Paint roller, 2" (5 cm) wide
6. Heavy red, green, or blue cotton cloth, 40" x 20" (100 x 50 cm)
7. Fabric paints (black and yellow)
8. 2 plastic or Styrofoam trays

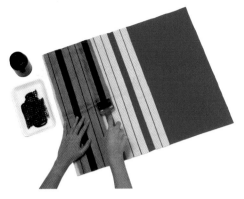

**1** Place strips of masking tape on the cloth to guide you in applying the paint. Start with a strip across the short edge of the cloth. Place the next strip 0.1" (0.25 cm) from the first strip and the next strip 1" (2.5 cm) from the second strip. Repeat these steps the whole length of the cloth, so there are two thin lines between each thick line, as in the picture above.

**2** Using the large paint roller, apply black paint over the entire cloth. When the paint is dry, peel off the masking tape. Repeat steps one and two starting across the long edge of the cloth.

**3** Place masking tape 0.5" (1.2 cm) from the edge across the short side of the cloth. Place another strip 0.1" (0.25 cm) from the first strip, and a third strip next to that. Leave no space between the second and third strips. Repeat these steps the whole length of the cloth, so there is a thin line on each side of every thick black line.

**4** Using the small paint roller, apply yellow paint over the entire cloth. When the paint is dry, peel off the masking tape. Repeat steps three and four across the long side of the cloth. Now, you have your own tartan sash!

# MAKE SCOTTISH SHORTBREAD

T he Scots are famous for their shortbread, a crisp, buttery, rich biscuit eaten as a snack with tea or after dinner. Shortbread is easy to make and tastes delicious. It is traditionally served broken into bite-sized pieces.

**You will need:**
1. Electric mixer
2. Oven mitt
3. Mixing bowl
4. Measuring cup
5. Baking pan
6. 2 oz. (60 g) ground rice flour
7. 4 oz. (115 g) butter
8. Cutting board
9. 4 oz. (115 g) white flour
10. 2 oz. (60 g) sugar
11. Wooden spoon
12. Fork

**1** Have an adult help you preheat the oven to 350°F (180 °C). Cream the butter with the electric mixer until it starts to take on a pale appearance. Gradually add sugar, beating the mixture until it is light and fluffy.

**2** Slowly add the flour to the mixture and knead for about five minutes to form a stiff dough.

**3** Spread the dough in the baking pan. Flatten it with the heel of your hand until it evenly covers the bottom.

**4** Use the fork to prick the surface of the dough at regular intervals, so the shortbread will be crispy. Ask an adult to place the dough in the oven for eight to ten minutes. Then, reduce the heat to 300°F (150°C) and bake for another 10 to 15 minutes until the shortbread is crisp and golden. Cool before serving, and you have a delicious Scottish treat!

# GLOSSARY

**aura**, 23 — Light or radiance.

**brooch**, 27 — A piece of jewelry with a pin at the back.

**Celts**, 4 — Ancient people from central and western Europe.

**civilian**, 19 — People or things that are not related to the military.

**climax**, 22 — The most exciting or important part of an event, which usually occurs near the end of the event.

**congregate**, 24 — Assemble, or gather together, to form a group.

**entourage**, 25 — Attendants, assistants, servants, and other people who travel with an important person.

**esplanade**, 19 — A wide, open space of level ground.

**Gaelic**, 4 — A language spoken by people in areas of Scotland and Ireland.

**navigational**, 21 — Related to the steering or directing of a ship or aircraft.

**pagan**, 24 — Beliefs and activities not related to any major world religion, usually including the belief in many gods.

**prevalent**, 21 — Widely practiced or accepted.

# INDEX

**Picture credits**
ANA: 7 (top), 12 (bottom), 14 (top); British Tourist Authority/Singapore: 22 (top); Camera Press: 12 (top), 27; Focus Team/Italy: 7 (bottom); The Hutchison Library: 3 (bottom), 16 (right), 19; International Photobank: 26; Life File: 24 (both), 25; Photobank Photolibrary: 4, 6, 8, 9 (bottom), 11 (bottom), 16 (left), 17; David Simson: 20 (both), 21, 22 (bottom), 23; Travel Ink: 18, 28; Trip Photographic Library: 1, 2, 3 (top), 5, 9 (top), 10, 11 (top), 13, 14 (bottom), 15

Digital scanning by Superskill Graphics Pte Ltd.